Ingredients

A large dollop of fun
Several spoons of common sense
A portion of imagination
A dose of preparation
A pinch of your inner child
A sprinkling of order
A large cup of love

Method

Combine the preparation and order in a large bowl until smooth. Then, using little spoons, forks and fingers, whisk together the common sense, imagination and inner child until the mixture is colourful and full of enthusiasm. Mix the fun and love together in a separate bowl then slowly fold into the colorful, enthusiastic batter. Pour the mixture into a beautiful, yet simple, mould and pop it in the oven. Refer to it regularly while your children are growing up then hold onto it until you have grandchildren, and refer to it again.

by Hannah Bennett

Notes:

Oven temperatures were tested in a conventional oven. Please adjust if you're using a fan oven. The recipes were tested using metric measurements. I have shown these measurements in a North American format in brackets, but it is not always possible to convert precisely, especially with Cups. The time shown in the clocks is the approximate time it will take to do the adult preparation and cooking together sections—ie. all the hands-on bits. If you want the total time until the food is ready, you will need to add on any cooking or chilling time.

Text copyright 2013 Annabel Woolmer
Illustrations copyright 2014 John Woolmer
Photography copyright 2014 Annabel Woolmer

Published in the United Kingdom by Tickle Fingers Publishing in 2014

ISBN: 978 0 9931111 0 5

The Tickle Fingers Cookbook

recipes & tips
for cooking with a toddler

by Annabel Woolmer

to my Mum for teaching me, to Eve and Zoë
for their enthusiasm and to John, with love.

Introduction

If you are looking for a recipe book with innovative new recipes to wow a dinner party, this is not the book for you. If you want simple, tasty recipes that your toddler can cook and have fun with, then this is it. Tickle Fingers is a recipe book for parents, grandparents and carers to use to cook with a toddler aged one to four years old, and beyond. It includes 30 recipes, 15 savoury and 15 sweet; ideas on how to make it safe and fun; and tips on techniques and tackling common problems. All the recipes are designed to be age-appropriate, easy-to-follow, and provide yummy, low-cost food that everyone, especially the little chef, will enjoy.

Some of you might already be sold on the idea of cooking with children as young as one. I suspect some of you might be wondering whether it's such a good idea. I started to cook with my children when they were about 13 months old on an experimental whim. I found that, with the right recipes, they could not only do it, but loved it. Amongst other things, I believe cooking at a very young age has given them:

Respect for food and the provider
A meal does not magically appear for them to accept or reject. Their direct involvement, or even just awareness of what goes into preparing a meal, gives them an interest in the outcome.

A positive response to food and eating
I am convinced that cooking has increased their interest in food and therefore willingness to try new things.

Fine motor skills and concentration
I don't know what difference it would have made had I not cooked with them. But watching my 2-year-old carefully spoon flour into a bowl without spilling

any convinced me that it was doing something for her focus and dexterity.

A sense of personal achievement
They love the idea that they've made something themselves for us all to enjoy. We always make a big play of thanking whoever was the little chef, just like they have to thank Mum or Dad for their meal.

Fun Time
It is always a struggle to find time to do fun things together. I know I am always promising them we'll get the paints out 'tomorrow' only to find it's the end of the week and I still haven't. It does take longer, but by involving them, we are doing something fun and constructive which needed doing anyway.

There are plenty of downsides: the mess; the perpetual conflict over when they can and can not lick the spoon; having to manage the super-keen budding chef who wants to help in the kitchen all the time. But for me the positives far out weigh the negatives.

When I started to cook with my eldest at 13 months, I hunted high and low to find something to help and inspire me. I found plenty of 'first' cookbooks, recipes for cooking with children, and even books for cooking with toddlers. But everything I found seemed appropriate only for cooking with over 3s or even older, or was about cooking for children, not with them. In the end, I made it up as I went along. It has been a steep learning curve. I made plenty of mistakes and made lots of things harder than they should have been.

This book brings together my experiences, and aims to make it as easy as possible to cook with a toddler. The recipes are presented in groups graded by difficulty (First Recipes, Gaining Confidence, and Budding Little Chef) to help you identify the most appropriate recipes to try with your child. While the later recipes are more challenging —more ingredients, take longer or need more dexterity—every recipe is suitable for a toddler. Each one has a limited number of achievable steps. There is no cooking on the hob (stovetop), no use of sharp knives, and no handling of raw meat.

I believe the key to cooking with a very young child is *preparation* and maintaining momentum. This is why each recipe has a section for you to do first, before involving the "little chef." This includes equipment and ingredients to lay out, and any cooking preparation which would be difficult or unsafe for a young child to do. This "Adult Prep" section is designed to set you up so that once you start, the child is involved in everything until the dish goes into the oven, fridge, or onto the table.

Cooking with a young child is not just about what goes on in the kitchen, there's the shopping and paying for the ingredients too. I have intentionally used good-value, *easy-to-find ingredients*. You won't have to spend hours searching for something in an obscure supermarket aisle while you and your little one have a melt down.

I hope this book will be a useful source of ideas or even the impetus to start cooking with a toddler.

Good Luck!

Contents

When to start

A child needs to be able to:

Understand basic commands, like "put those into there."

Be walking steadily with reasonable hand control.

This could range from 1 year to 18 months, or beyond. If you're not sure, give it a try. You can always abandon and return to it when they're older. But don't expect too much. At the beginning you will probably have to step in a lot, especially with the very young. At any age, you might have to try it several times before they start to get the idea. I would say that between 1 and 2 you are simply preparing the ground and having fun. Between 2 and 3 is when, with practice, they are able to start cooking for themselves with minimal help.

What you need

Very little. There is no need to buy lots of children's kitchen equipment. They can use most of what you have already. However, here are some suggestions to make it easier and safer.

Small, low table
Anything the right height for them to stand up at easily. You can also use the base of a chair, but you might find the lack of space annoying. I would not advise having your toddler standing on a stool or chair at the worktop. You don't want to spend the whole time worrying about them falling.

Plastic or stainless steel mixing bowls
This will depend on your child's temperament. My eldest was so careful, I was relaxed about using Pyrex mixing bowls. When I tried cooking with my youngest, I quickly decided there was a strong probability that the bowl would end up on the floor in a fit of enthusiasm. So I bought plastic.

Child-safe knives
A table knife is sufficient for all the recipes in this book. However, if you have an older toddler who wants to get more involved in food preparation, then you can buy child-safe knives that cut through more easily.

Flour dredger
Fun for sprinkling flour on a surface or rolling pin to stop sticking.

Non-stick baking mat
You can get these in different bright colours. They provide a hygienic surface to prepare food on, and when baking are easier to use than greaseproof (waxed) paper.

Handle grater

The sort of thing where you put the cheese in the top and wind the handle to grate. However, this is only worth getting for an older toddler who is going to able to wind the handle. You can also buy handle peelers/choppers for apples and potatoes, and others for finely chopping herbs.

Apron

Mainly because they get so excited about putting it on, which helps set the tone.

Take a look at www.cookwithtoddlers.com if you want more information on any of the above.

How to engage your toddler

Choose your recipe carefully

This book has lots of recipe ideas but you can also adapt recipes from adult books. Keep these principles in mind:

The shorter the better. 6 ingredients and about 5-6 steps is the limit you can expect from most toddlers.

In the early days, try to avoid ingredients you don't want your toddler to eat: raw egg, raw meats etc. It might take them time to learn not to stuff everything in their mouths. If it's something they shouldn't eat, then it gets stressful rather than fun.

Avoid cooking on the hob (stovetop) As they can not do that safely, they have to watch and wait. And, as with most things with toddlers, keeping up the momentum is key. The ideal recipe involves a few steps to assemble, and then into the oven or fridge.

Avoid expensive ingredients. This is more for your well-being than your child's. In this book I have tried to use good-value, everyday ingredients. You want to feel able to let your child loose on the food. I know I wouldn't feel able to do that with something like an expensive piece of fresh salmon.

Don't choose a recipe by pretty pictures alone. The pictures of the food in this book are fairly ordinary. This is intentional. My pet peeve with children's cookbooks is the use of pictures of decorated food designed to attract children, but which they haven't a hope of recreating. My daughter picks recipes because she likes the look of "the little bees" or "happy faces" and is then disappointed when the end result doesn't look anything like the picture.

Lay everything out before you start

This seems obvious, but I still find myself rummaging around to find a key ingredient while the children get bored and start mucking about with everything I've already got out. Chaos, stress and momentum gone!

It is also an idea to fill a sink or bowl with soapy water with a towel handy so you can clean hands if and when necessary without having to break away from cooking. Or you could use wipes.

Get them to do as much as possible

This ties in with choosing the right recipes; ones where they are able to stay involved throughout. Having said that, you will almost certainly need to step in to finish a task and move it on to the next stage. For example, a toddler's idea of mixing is usually to prod it a few times. Encourage them to do more, show them what to do, encourage again, and then help them to move on.

Avoid noisy kitchen gadgets

There are quicker and more effective ways to do many of the recipes in this book by using electric whisks, food processors etc. And in the right context, using an electric gadget can be fun for a child. However, I have tried, where possible, to avoid them. Firstly because it makes the recipes much more hands on. And secondly, because many very young children don't like, or are even scared of, the noise these gadgets make.

Timing, timing, timing

Picking the right time to cook with a young child is important. I have a tendency to decide just before lunch that we'll make something nice for pudding. Consequently we are in a rush, they are hungry, and it all goes wrong. Try to make sure you have time with minimal distractions, and try to avoid cooking with them when they are hungry. They are going to struggle to concentrate if all they want to do is eat what is in front of them.

Talk to them

Talk to them. Find as many ways you can to describe what they have to do; the sillier the better. For example, mixing with a wooden spoon could be : 'a helicopter,' 'a horse on a carousel,' 'burying treasure under sand (flour),' or 'driving around a race track.' Sing a song which goes with the action e.g. "round and round the garden" for mixing. Or make a little song up - it doesn't have to be a musical masterpiece! Use this opportunity to talk to them about the food; where it came from, its colour, its texture, its taste. It will all help them to understand what they are supposed to be doing and stay engaged.

Don't go for perfection

To me, the most important thing about cooking with a child is that you have fun and end up with something tasty to enjoy together at the end. Don't worry too much about doing every stage perfectly, or making the final result look dinner-party worthy. The recipes in this book are intentionally robust and forgiving. They allow for a bit of dropped flour here, or lump of butter there.

Stay calm

This is easier said than done when food is going everywhere, your toddler is trying to eat flour and the phone rings. But the most important thing is that it is meant to be fun for you both. If it isn't, stop and try again another time.

Think about schemas

A member of staff in one of our local Sure Start Centres introduced me to the concept of schemas. The general idea is that toddlers learn through different ways of playing known as schemas. Some toddlers have an obvious tendency towards a certain schema. Others tend towards several schemas and/or tend towards different ones at different stages. If you spot your child emphasising a schema in their play, then you can tailor how you present cooking to them accordingly.

When I first started cooking with her, my eldest was a 'transporter.' She would happily while away hours carrying things from one place to another and push around her baby pushchair. So I used to get her to do a lot of moving ingredients from one bowl to another. My youngest was an 'enveloper.' She liked to cover paper and hands (!) in paint and hide under blankets. So I liked to do recipes which involved wrapping things up (eg. samosas or wraps), or getting her hands into the mixture (eg. salmon paste).

Here is a brief overview of the main schemas and ideas for applying them to cooking.

	what you might see in their play	cooking tasks they might like	particularly appropriate recipes
transporting	pushing things around; carrying things	moving ingredients from place to place	all
trajectory	throwing, kicking, climbing, pouring	pouring liquid & spooning ingredients, especially from height	biscuit cake, frittata, choc cake, bread & butter pud
connecting	jigsaws; building blocks; sequencing; or laying things out	constructing dishes	pizza, chicken baskets, rainbow salad, apple cake
transforming	adding things to change them eg. water to sand	mixing ingredients that change texture or colour	biscuit cake, lollies, fruity mess, cheesecake
enveloping	hiding, wrapping, layering, covering things or selves	getting hands into mixture, "burying" ingredients	salmon paste, samosas, muffins, fishcakes, crumble
containing	filling and emptying things, climbing into boxes	putting ingredients into things	pittas, yoghurt pots, samosas, chicken baskets
rotating	interest in things that go round: wheels, roundabouts	mixing, whisking, rolling things up	all

Tips

1. Softening butter: what to do if you forget to take it out of the fridge, or don't have time to let it go soft naturally

   Some of the recipes need softened butter. You need the butter to be soft—able to squish between fingers—so that a young child can combine it with another ingredient. However, it is important to soften butter gently. Do not just whack it in the microwave or on the hob (stovetop). This will change the properties of the butter, and might make the recipe fail. If you have a microwave, heat the butter at 10-20% of its maximum power for 20 seconds at a time. Every 20 seconds, turn the butter so it softens evenly. You will probably have to do this 4-6 times depending on how hard the butter was.

2. Spooning sticky ingredients from one place to another

   The best way to do this is with two spoons, preferably metal. Get your child to put a spoon in each hand. Get them to scoop with one and scrape off the mixture with the other. If they struggle with this then you could do one spoon, and they could do the other. I find it useful and fun to get them to name the spoons: 'Topsy & Tim,' 'Jack & Jill,' 'Peter & Paul' etc. That way I can more easily explain what they are supposed to be doing with each spoon: e.g. 'scoop up the mixture with Topsy' and 'scrape the mixture with Tim.'

3. Breaking eggs without getting shell in the mixture

   You need to get them to pull the egg apart rather than crush it in their hands. To encourage this, I usually say a silly rhyme - "knock, knock on the door and open." Whilst singing this, I get them to knock the egg on the rim of the bowl, and then pull the two halves of the egg open.

④ Combining butter and sugar

The key to this with a very young child is to have the butter as soft as possible otherwise they will not be strong enough. Get them to squash the butter with the back of a wooden spoon and then stir. Keep doing a 'squash and stir' action. You might have to finish this off, especially if the butter is a little too hard. Recipes often call for butter and sugar to be mixed until 'soft and fluffy.' The recipes in this book are robust enough that you don't need to worry about this; just get them combined.

⑤ Turning flour and butter into crumbs for pastry or crumble

You want them to rub the flour into the butter with their finger tips rather than squishing it together with their hands. If they do the latter, they could end up with a lump of dough rather than crumbs. To encourage them to use their finger tips, I tell them to pretend they are tickling the butter into the flour. We call it 'tickle fingers.'"

⑥ Cutting

I strongly recommend that you never use a sharp knife, even if you are cutting with your child. I used to use one occasionally and hold the knife with them. And then one day in a moment of absent mindedness I put the knife down within reach of my 2 year old. She made a grab for it. Luckily she didn't hurt herself but I learnt my lesson. Now I do any cutting that needs a sharp knife and put it away before I get my children in the kitchen to cook.

However, cutting is a useful skill for your toddler to learn. The recipes in this book allow your toddler to practise cutting soft foods with a blunt table knife or a child-safe knife. Get them to tuck their thumb in when they hold the food. I tell my children to 'hide' their thumb in their hand. With the knife in the other hand, get them to do a sawing action forwards and backwards whilst pushing down on the food. For obvious reasons this task needs close supervision, and you will probably still need to hold the knife and food with your child long after they have mastered most other cooking skills.

⑦ Bringing dough together

Unlike when making crumble, you want them to get their hands in and squish. The heat of their hands will help to combine the mixture. None of these recipes require full-on kneading. Just get them to take as big a handful as possible, and squish and squeeze until it comes together.

⑧ Rolling things out

Make sure you have prepared the area and rolling pin with a good sprinkling of flour to prevent sticking. If you have a flour dredger then your child can have fun making it 'snow' everywhere.

The biggest mistake children make is to grip the rolling pin so that their fingers are in the way when they roll. Encourage them to spread their fingers out while they roll. I tell my children to make 'stars' or a 'butterfly' with their hands.

We have children's rolling pins which they use for play dough, but I prefer them to use a big, adult one for cooking. I think it is easier for them to use because they have room to spread their hands out, and the weight helps them to compress the dough as they roll. Do not be surprised if your child struggles with rolling. Although a favourite in children's cookbooks, it is actually a hard thing for very young children to manage as it takes coordination and strength.

⑨ Pinching

If your child needs to pick up a pinch of flour or other ingredient to sprinkle it, get them to make a 'duck' or a 'parrot' with their hand. Get them to put their fingers and thumb together in a 'quack' or 'squawk.' Then get them to do the same action to pick up the flour. Then get them to rub their thumb over their fingers to sprinkle.

Trouble-shooting

"When I try to cook with my daughter, she just wants to eat all the time. And when I won't let her because it's raw batter, she just gets upset."

I think this is the number one problem when cooking with very young children. You want them to be interested in the ingredients. You want them to be trying everything they can. But you don't want them sticking their hands in and eating things like raw egg. They don't understand when it's ok to eat and when it's not. So they get confused and upset.

Find a time when she's not hungry, eg. just after snack-time. Explain clearly that she can try things when you say it is ok. If you're cooking with something you don't want her to eat, like cake batter with raw egg, put out a bowl of something she can eat, like raisins. If she tries to eat the batter, direct her to the bowl and say you can try that. Let her try as many of the ingredients as possible. But when you do, make a big thing of saying 'you can try this' so she learns it is ok when you give things to her, but not ok just to take stuff.

To try to avoid this problem, none of the 'first recipes' for very young children in this book contain anything they can't try.

"My son loves cooking. He wants to do it all the time. Sometimes I just need to get on with doing dinner but he gets upset if I don't let him help me."

You don't want to dampen his enthusiasm, but there will be plenty of times when you are doing things he can't help with. Try finding little things he can do to help, even if it's just putting cutlery on the table. I sometimes cut up the vegetables and then just get my daughter to put them into the pans (before they've been on the heat!).

You could also try setting up a pretend kitchen. This doesn't have to be an expensive, shop-bought one: a cardboard box for an oven, some spare pots and pans etc. He can then be 'pretend' cooking while you get on with the real thing.

"My son doesn't like getting his hands messy."

Some children do not like messy play. However, cooking could be a way for him to gain confidence with it. Chose recipes which don't involve sticking hands in, or do this bit for him. Get him using spoons to move ingredients around. Don't push it. If your child's fear is extreme, get expert advice.

"I really want to cook with my children but I can't stand the idea of the mess."

Young children are going to make a mess, but I always think it's amazing how little they actually make. If you invest in a small low table and keep all the cooking your child does on that, any mess will be contained in one place. Nothing a quick wipe and sweep won't fix. You could even place a mat or oil cloth under the table to gather up any spills.

If you're still worried, once you've done the adult preparation stage, none of these recipes require you to be in the kitchen. You could lay out everything somewhere you don't mind getting messy, even outside.

A note on timings. I have included a clock with an approximate time each recipe will take to prepare, both adult preparation and cooking together - ie. everything up to the point it goes into the oven or fridge. But these timings will vary a lot depending on the age and speed of your child. Something a 3-year old might do in a minute could take an 18-month old 5 minutes or more.

Recipes

salmon paste p30

curried chicken wraps p28

ham & mushroom pizza p29

sausage pasta bake p31

tuna pitta pockets p32

First Recipes

for those just starting out or very young

Curried Chicken Wraps

makes 4 half wraps

An easy recipe for using up leftover chicken. Serve with some sliced cucumber and tomatoes for a quick lunch, or wrap up and take on a picnic. A fun recipe for teaching your child about tastes like bitter, sweet, and spicy. You could put a little lime, mango chutney, and (a very little!) curry powder on their tongue for them to taste the differences.

Ingredients

- 120g (4oz) cooked chicken
- 1 heaped tablespoon greek yoghurt
- 1 heaped tablespoon mayonnaise
- 1/4 level teaspoon mild curry powder
- 1 heaped teaspoon mango chutney
- Small lime quarter
- 2 wraps

Adult Prep

- Cut a small lime in quarters, or eigths if lime is large
- Lay out: ingredients, mixing bowl, 2 tablespoons, table knife, chopping board, and kitchen foil (optional).

Together

1 Tear chicken into smallish pieces. Put in bowl.

2 Add Greek yoghurt, mayonnaise, curry powder & mango chutney to bowl.

3 Squeeze juice from lime quarter into bowl. Mix with tablespoon until all combined.

4 Spoon half the mixture onto wrap & spread it out.

5 Roll up wrap & cut in half with table knife.

6 Repeat with other wrap. If not eating straight away, wrap in kitchen foil.

Ham & Mushroom Pizza

makes 1 small pizza

This recipe is for a ham & mushroom pizza, but you could use any toppings you like. This doesn't need much adult input, even with very young children, which makes it a great starter recipe. They are best eaten straight from oven. However you can prepare in advance, cover in cling film (wrap) and leave in fridge for a few hours until you're ready to cook.

Ingredients

- 1 flour tortilla
- 1 tablespoon ready-made tomato pasta sauce
- 50g (1/4 cup) cooked ham
- 50g (1/2 cup) mushrooms
- 100g (1 cup) fresh mozzarella
- 2 large basil leaves (optional)
- 1 tablespoon olive oil

Adult Prep

- Preheat oven to 200C/390F/Gas 6.
- Put olive oil in a saucer.
- Lay out: ingredients, baking tray & 2 table spoons

Together

1 Put tortilla on tray. Spoon tomato sauce onto tortilla & spread out with back of spoon.

2 Tear ham & mushrooms into small pieces. Scatter on top of tortilla.

3 Tear mozzarella & basil leaves & scatter on tortilla.

4 Gently tip saucer to drizzle olive oil over top.

And finally... bake in oven for 8 minutes

Salmon Paste

serves 4

This is a fun recipe for children who like to get their hands mucky. If you or they don't like the idea of sticking their hands in, then they can use a fork to mush the salmon. Delicious spread on cold toast or crackers. Will keep up to 4 days in an airtight container in the fridge.

Ingredients

- 170g (5oz) tin (can) of boneless salmon
- 2 heaped tablespoons cream cheese
- 30ml (2tbsp) cream
- 1/2 teaspoon tomato paste
- 1/8 teaspoon of paprika
- Lemon quarter

Adult Prep

- Open salmon tin (can) & drain off liquid.
- Cut lemon into quarters.
- Lay out: ingredients, mixing bowl, 2 tablespoons, fork & pot or container with lid.

Together

1. Scrape salmon into bowl. Mush with hands until broken up.

2. Spoon cream cheese into bowl and mush into salmon with hands.

3. Add cream, tomato paste and paprika.

4. Squeeze lemon quarter so juice goes into bowl. Mix until all combined.

5. Spoon into container.

Sausage Pasta Bake

serves 4

A useful recipe if, like me, you often cook more pasta than you need. Put excess pasta in an airtight container in the fridge for up to 2 days. If you cook extra sausages in advance to use in this recipe, let them cool completely, wrap in foil and put in fridge for up to 3 days. If you have a handle grater then children can also help grate the cheese.

Ingredients

- 400g (4 cups) cooked fusilli or penne pasta (200g dried pasta, cooked)
- 3 cooked sausages
- 1 bell pepper
- 6 heaped tablespoons readymade tomato pasta sauce
- 150g (1 1/2cups) cheddar cheese

Adult Prep

- Slice bell pepper into thin slices.
- Grate cheddar cheese.
- Preheat oven to 220C/425F/Gas 7.
- Lay out: ingredients, oven-proof dish, 2 tablespoons, mixing bowl, table knife & chopping board.

Together

1 Put pasta & sliced peppers into bowl.

2 Add pasta sauce & mix.

3 Cut sausages into chunks with table knife. Add to bowl & mix.

4 Spoon mixture into oven-proof dish.

5 Sprinkle over grated cheese.

And finally... bake in oven for 15-20 minutes until cheese is melted & sizzling.

Tuna Mayo Pitta Pockets

6 half pittas

These are a lunch-time favourite in our house. You can prepare them in advance and then warm just before eating. They are also good without cooking, perfect for a picnic. If you have a handle grater, then children can also help grate the cheese.

Ingredients

- x2 160g (5oz) tins (cans) of tuna
- 2 heaped tablespoons mayonnaise
- 50g (1/4cup) tinned (canned) sweetcorn
- 100g (1 cup) cheddar cheese
- 6 half pittas

Adult Prep

- Open tuna and sweetcorn tins (cans) & drain off liquid.
- Grate cheddar cheese.
- Preheat oven to 180C/350F/Gas 4.
- Lay out: ingredients, mixing bowl, 2 tablespoons, fork & baking tray.

Together

1 Scrape tuna into mixing bowl. Mush with hands or fork until broken up.

2 Spoon mayonnaise into bowl & mush into tuna with hands or fork.

3 Add sweetcorn & mix with tablespoon.

4 Spoon or use hands to put 2 heaped tablespoons of tuna mix into each pitta half.

5 Use hands to shove a handful of grated cheese inside each pitta half.

6 Put on baking tray.

And finally... warm in oven for 5 minutes. Eat straight away.

frozen yoghurt lollies p36

chocolate fork biscuits p35

fruity yoghurt pots p37

chocolate fork biscuits

Chocolate Biscuit Cake

makes 12 slices

I have broken my own advice about not using the hob (stovetop) here because the hob part can be done beforehand so your child isn't waiting around. The final step will give them possibly the best chocolatey fingers they've ever had to lick. If you or they don't want sticky hands, then put the greaseproof paper on before they press down. Will keep up to 5 days in fridge.

Ingredients

- Teaspoon of butter for greasing
- 300g (10oz) digestive biscuits (graham crackers)
- 75g (1/2cup) raisins
- 180g (6oz) butter
- 50g (1/2cup) cocoa powder
- 120g (4oz) golden syrup

Adult Prep

- Gently melt butter, cocoa powder & golden syrup together in a pan. Transfer into a jug.
- Lay out: remaining ingredients, 20 cm spring bottomed cake tin (pan), 2 tablespoons, mixing bowl & greaseproof (waxed) paper or a baking mat.

Together

1 Rub teaspoon of butter all over cake tin to grease it. Set aside.

2 Break digestives into bits; not too small; one biscuit into about six pieces. Put biscuit bits into bowl.

3 Add raisins to bowl & mix with tablespoon.

4 Pour melted syrup mixture onto biscuits & mix until biscuits bits covered.

5 Spoon mixture into cake tin.

6 Spread mixture out & press down with hands to make a compressed flat top.

And finally... cover top with greaseproof paper & put in fridge for minimum 2 hours. Cut into cake slices to serve.

Chocolate Fork Biscuits

makes 16 biscuits

These were the first things I made with both my girls when they were about 13-14 months old. My mother used to make them with me. They are a great biscuit (cookie) for children with egg or dairy allergies. For the latter, substitute butter with dairy-free spread or margarine. Will keep for up to 1 week in an airtight container.

Ingredients

- Teaspoon of butter for greasing (or use baking mat)
- 110g (4oz) butter
- 60g (4tbsp) sugar
- 110g (1 cup) self-raising flour
- 30g (4tbsp) cocoa powder

Adult Prep

- Take butter out of fridge at least an hour before cooking to soften.
- Preheat oven to 180C/350F/Gas 4.
- Lay out: ingredients, baking tray, large mixing bowl, wooden spoon, 2 tablespoons, glass of water & fork.

Together

1 Rub teaspoon of butter over baking tray to grease (or use a baking mat).

2 Put butter & sugar into bowl & squish & stir with wooden spoon until well combined.

3 Add flour & cocoa powder & mix until combined. Don't worry if mix is dry, squish together with hands.

4 Take out walnut-sized lumps & roll into balls. Put balls onto baking tray - spaced out because they will spread.

5 Lightly press top of each ball with fork. If mixture sticks to fork, dip fork into cup of water between balls.

And finally... bake in oven for 9 minutes. Leave to cool on tray.

Frozen Yoghurt Lollies

makes 6 lollies

Healthy, tasty lollies which are easy to make. You can make all sorts of flavours and flavour combinations by using different fruits and flavoured yoghurts. I find it a useful recipe for using up fruit which has gone a bit squishy. Childen love squashing the fruit and making pink swirls in the yoghurt.

Ingredients

- 40g (1/4cup) raspberries
- 125g (1/2cup) greek yoghurt
- 100g (1/2cup) raspberry or strawberry yoghurt
- 1/2 teaspoon Vanilla extract
- 50ml (4tbsp) cream

Adult Prep

- Put raspberries into a plastic freezer bag.
- Lay out: ingredients, 6 ice-lolly moulds, mixing bowl & 3 tablespoons.

Together

1. Put Greek yoghurt, flavoured yoghurt, vanilla extract & cream into bowl.

2. Hold plastic bag closed whilst child squishes raspberries inside with hands.

3. Add contents of bag to bowl & mix.

4. Spoon mixture into ice-lolly moulds.

And finally... freeze for a minimum of 2 hours.

Fruity Yoghurt Pots

serves 4

This is a quick dessert which you can get your child to put together at the table just before eating. However, if you want to make it in advance, keep the crushed digestives to one side and sprinkle on just before eating. Otherwise they will go soggy. If you get them to add the sliced banana and/or blueberries one at a time, this is a good recipe for a bit of counting practice.

Ingredients

- 1 banana
- approx 30 blueberries
- 3 digestive biscuits (graham crackers)
- 8 heaped tablespoons plain yoghurt

Adult Prep

- Lay out: ingredients, 4 small plastic cups, 2 tablespoons, mixing bowl, small mixing bowl, table knife & chopping board.

Together

1 Cut banana into slices with table knife. Put into mixing bowl.

2 Add blueberries to bowl.

3 Add yogurt to bowl & mix.

4 Divide mixture into plastic cups..

5 Crush digestives between fingers over small bowl until in little pieces/big crumbs.

6 Sprinkle digestive crumbs generously onto top of each cup & serve.

Shortbread

makes 15-20 slices or fingers

This is a classic and, as with all classic recipes, there are many ways to make it. A small child can make this version with little adult input. Personally, I don't think it needs it, but if you want to be traditional, then sprinkle some caster sugar on top just after it comes out of the oven. Will keep in an airtight container for up to 1 week.

Ingredients

- Teaspoon of butter for greasing
- 250g (8oz) butter
- 125g (2/3cup) brown sugar
- 375g (3 3/4cups) plain (all-purpose) flour

Adult Prep

- Take butter out of fridge at least 1 hour before using to soften.
- Preheat oven to 170C/325F/Gas 3.
- Lay out: ingredients, 20cm round or square cake tin, large mixing bowl, tablespoon, wooden spoon & fork.

Together

1. Rub teaspoon of butter all over cake tin to grease it. Set aside.

2. Put butter & sugar into bowl & squish & stir with wooden spoon until well combined.

3. Mix in flour until just combined. Don't worry if it looks crumbly.

4. Put mixture into tin. Spread & pat down as if you were making a sand castle.

5. Prick dough all over with a fork.

And finally... bake in oven for 40 minutes until light brown. Cut into portions while still warm in the tin. Then leave to cool before removing.

fruity yoghurt pots p37

chocolate fork biscuits p35

chocolate biscuit cake p34

shortbread p38

chicken bread baskets p42

guacamole p44

rainbow salad p45

frittata p43

Gaining Confidence
for those with a bit of experience

Chicken Bread Baskets

makes 12 mini baskets

These look and taste great. Serve with a salad for lunch or these also make great party food for adults and children. You can put anything in these bread baskets. The Salmon Paste on page 30 makes a good filler. If you're wondering what to do with the leftover bits of bread - blitz them in a food processor to make breadcrumbs and freeze until ready to use.

Ingredients

- 2 tablespoons of olive oil
- 6 slices of white or wholemeal bread
- 120g (4oz) cooked chicken
- 2 heaped tablespoons mayonnaise
- Teaspoon of tarragon or parsley
- Teaspoon mustard
- Pinch of paprika

Adult Prep

- Chop teaspoon of fresh tarragon or use dried.
- Preheat oven to 180C/350F/Gas 4.
- Lay out: ingredients: cupcake tray, pastry brush, 68mm(2 3/4") round cookie cutter, mixing bowl, tablespoon, 2 teaspoons & cooling rack.

Together

1 Cut 2 circles of bread from each slice with cookie cutter, making 12 circles.

2 Squash & press each bread circle with hands until flat. Brush each circle with oil using pastry brush.

3 Place each circle into cupcake tray & press down with fingers to make basket shapes.

Bake baskets in oven for 10 minutes until light brown and crisp. Remove from tray & cool on cooling rack.

4 Whilst bread baskets are cooking & cooling, tear chicken into small pieces.

5 Put chicken, mayonnaise, tarragon, mustard & small sprinkling of paprika into mixing bowl & mix.

6 When chicken baskets are cold, spoon mixture into them & serve.

Frittata

serves 6

This is a great recipe for using up leftover vegetables, especially potatoes. I just use whatever I have available from supper the night before. Frittata is best eaten warm or at room temperature. It makes a good alternative to sandwiches on picnics; just cut into slices and wrap in foil. If you're not eating within 12 hours, you should put in fridge.

Adult Prep

- Grate cheddar cheese.
- Preheat the oven to 180C/350F/Gas 4.
- Lay out: ingredients, oven-proof dish or pan, pastry brush, fork, large mixing bowl, chopping board & table knife.

Ingredients

- 280g (2 1/2cups) cooked mixed vegetables of your choice eg. potatoes, peppers, peas, broccoli, courgettes (zucchini), onions.
- 6 eggs
- 3 tablespoons olive oil, plus 1 to grease
- 200ml (1 cup) milk
- 120g (1 cup) grated cheddar cheese
- Salt & pepper

Together

1 Brush tablespoon of oil onto oven-proof dish with pastry brush to grease.

2 Break eggs into mixing bowl. Add milk & olive oil. Whisk together with fork.

3 Cut cooked vegetables into small chunks with table knife. Add to bowl.

4 Add grated cheese & mix together with fork.

5 Pour mixture into oven-proof dish.

And finally... Season & bake in oven for 30-40 minutes until golden & firm.

Guacamole

Serves 6-8 as a dip

While making this, I talk to my children about the colours (purple avocado skins, green avocado flesh, red tomatoes) and about the textures (hard avocado stone, soft avocado flesh, smooth tomato skin, rough avocado skin). This recipe is intentionally mild so children will enjoy the result, especially with some tortilla chips. Will keep in an airtight container in fridge for 3-4 days.

Ingredients

- 2 small or 1 large avocado
- 2 cherry tomatoes
- 1 large or 2 small garlic cloves
- Half a small lime
- Small pinch of paprika
- Small pinch of salt

Adult Prep

- Cut 2 cherry tomatoes into half.
- Peel garlic cloves.
- Cut avocados in half & throw away stones.
- Lay out: ingredients; large mixing bowl, fork or potato masher, tablespoon, chopping board, garlic press, bowl or airtight container.

Together

1. Scoop out flesh from avocados with tablespoon & put in bowl.

2. Mash avocados with fork or potato masher.

3. Squash cherry tomatoes & garlic cloves through garlic press into bowl.

4. Squeeze over juice from lime half.

5. Add small pinch of paprika & salt. Mix thoroughly with fork.

6. Spoon into bowl or container.

Rainbow Salad

serves 6

I love doing this with my children, especially in the summer. It's easy. It's a fun way to talk about colours. And it gets them trying all sorts of healthy ingredients. My eldest has re-named it 'pirate treasure' salad and once mixed, likes to 'dig' for 'treasure' to find the bits she likes best. It could also be part of a project to introduce the idea of growing food. Quick growing lettuce germinates within 7-10 days and is ready to cut within weeks, so good for impatient toddlers. You can grow it indoors or outdoors in containers, harvest, and then get cooking.

Adult Prep

- Peel and finely chop carrot.
- Finely chop tomato.
- Put out all the salad ingredients on little plates or bowls.
- Lay out: dressing ingredients, large mixing bowl, 2 tablespoons & empty jam jar with lid.

Ingredients

- 1 large tomato
- 1 carrot
- 3 tablespoons tinned sweetcorn kernels
- 150g (2cups) mixed lettuce leaves
- 3 tablespoons blueberries
- 10 red grapes
- 100g (1 cup) mozzarella
- 100g (1/2cup) ham
- 3 tablespoons croutons
- Dressing: 3 tablespoons olive oil, teaspoon mustard, 1 tablespoon honey, teaspoon balsamic vinegar

Together

1 Put lettuce in bowl. Then let them loose on ingredients; trying stuff, adding what they want.

2 Stir with tablespoons.

3 Put dressing ingredients in jam jar. Put lid on tight & shake, shake, shake.

Vegetable Samosas

makes 6-8 samosas

There is a bit of adult preparation for these, especially if you don't have leftover vegetables to use. However, they are really fun to make, particularly for children who love to paint and wrap things up. Delicious served with a dollop of mango chutney to dip into. Don't worry if you don't end up with perfect triangles, as long as they are well wrapped up, they will work.

Adult Prep

- Finely chop onion & fry in teaspoon of butter on a medium heat until soft. A few minutes before you take onion off heat, stir in the garam masala.
- Preheat oven to 180C/350F/Gas 4.
- Lay out: ingredients, chopping board, table knife, mixing bowl, tablespoon, pastry brush & baking tray.

Ingredients

- 35g (1 small) cooked potato
- 25g (1 small) cooked carrot
- 25g (2tbsp) cooked green beans
- Half a small onion
- 1/2 teaspoon butter
- 1/2 teaspoon garam masala
- 25g (2tbsp) frozen peas
- 6 filo pastry sheets
- 4 tablespoons vegetable oil

Together

1. Cut cooked potato, carrot & beans into small chunks with table knife. Put in bowl.

2. Add frozen peas & cooked, spiced onions to bowl & mix well.

3. Lay out 1 sheet of filo pasty. Brush oil all over using pastry brush.

4. Fold filo sheet lengthways. Put spoonful of mixture in bottom right corner.

5. Fold bottom left corner over right hand edge. Fold bottom right corner to right edge. Keep folding until have a triangular parcel.

6. Brush parcel again with oil & put on baking tray. Repeat for each samosa.

And finally... bake in oven for 15-20 minutes until golden and crisp.

apple cake p48

fruity mess p51

vegetable samosas p46

vegetable samosas p46

Apple Cake

serves 6-8

This apple cake is an easier alternative to an apple crumble. Like crumble, it is best eaten warm with cream, custard or ice cream but is also lovely cold. You can keep in fridge for up to a week. I use an 'apple master' so the children can help me to peel, core and slice the apples by turning the handle. They enjoy seeing the apple skins spiral off the apples.

Ingredients

- 3 dessert apples
- Teaspoon of butter for greasing
- 125g (4oz) butter
- 125g (2/3cup) sugar
- 125g (1 1/4cup) self-raising flour
- 2 eggs

Adult Prep

- Peel, core & cut 3 dessert apples into slices.
- Take butter out of fridge at least 1 hour before using to soften.
- Preheat oven to 180C/350F/Gas 4.
- Lay out: ingredients, 20 cm round pie dish or cake tin (pan), large mixing bowl,

Together

1 Rub teaspoon of butter all over cake tin.

2 Lay apple slices out on bottom of tin. Set aside.

3 Put butter & sugar in mixing bowl & squish & stir with wooden spoon until combined.

4 Add eggs to bowl & mix.

5 Add flour to bowl & do a final mix until flour has been mixed in.

6 Spoon mixture onto apples & spread out with back of tablespoon.

And finally... bake in oven for 30 minutes until golden brown & springy to touch. Turn out onto a plate with apples on top.

Banana & Choc Chip Cakes

Makes 9

This is a great recipe for using up bananas that are getting too soft. They are fun to make as little cakes but you can also cook as one cake in a greased tin (pan). Will keep in an airtight container for 4 days.

Ingredients

- 1 ripe banana
- 50g (1/4 cup) sugar
- 50ml (4 tbsp) vegetable oil
- 1/2 tsp vanilla extract
- 1 egg
- 120g (1 cup) self-raising flour
- 100g (2/3 cup) chocolate chips

Adult Prep

- Preheat oven to 180C/350F/Gas 4.
- Lay out: ingredients, cupcake tray, 10 cupcake cases, mixing bowl, wooden spoon, fork or potato masher & 2 tablespoons.

Together

1. Put cupcake cases in tray & set aside.

2. Mash banana in mixing bowl with fork or potato masher.

3. Add oil, sugar, egg & vanilla extract to mashed banana & mix with wooden spoon.

4. Add flour, & chocolate chips & mix until combined.

5. Spoon mixture into cases until each is two-thirds full.

And finally... bake for 15-20 minutes until light brown and springy to touch.

Chocolate Cake Squares

makes 20 mini squares

No children's cookbook is complete without a chocolate cake recipe. This is an easy and versatile one. If your child is allergic to dairy then swap the milk for warm water and top with icing or jam. If they can't eat eggs, leave them out. I've chosen to make it square to make it easier to cut into child-size portions, but if you don't have a square tin, a round one will work.

Adult Prep

- Preheat oven to 180C/350F/Gas 4.
- Lay out: ingredients, large mixing bowl, hand whisk, pastry brush, 20-22cm(8") square cake tin (pan), spatula, cooling rack, table knife & table spoon.

Ingredients

- 160g (1 cup) self-raising flour
- 30g (4tbsp) cocoa powder
- 120g (2/3cup) sugar
- 1/4 teaspoon salt
- 100ml (1/2cup) milk
- 60ml (1/4cup) vegetable oil
- 2 eggs
- Teaspoon vanilla extract
- 100ml (1/2cup) warm water
- 3 tablespoons chocolate hazelnut spread

Together

1 Use pastry brush to paint a little oil over cake tin to grease.

2 Put all ingredients except for chocolate spread into bowl.

3 Mix well with hand whisk. Pour into cake tin.

Bake in oven for 30 mintues until springy to touch. Cool on cooling rack.

4 Dollop 3 generous tablespoons of chocolate spread onto cooled cake.

5 Spread over top of cake with table knife.

6 Use table knife to cut into small squares to serve.

Fruity Mess

serves 4

This is a version of Eton Mess. You can make with any fruit combinations you like. Swapping the banana for 60g blueberries works well. You can make your own meringues, but you will find ready-made meringue cases in most supermarkets.

Ingredients

- 150g (3/4 cup) strawberries
- 100ml (1/2 cup) whipping cream
- 100g (1/2 cup) greek yoghurt
- 4 meringues (or 1 large pavlova base)
- 1 banana

Adult Prep

- Hull and quarter strawberries. Put 100g into a plastic freezer bag. Set aside remaining 50g for decorating.
- Whip 100ml cream into soft peaks.
- Lay out: ingredients, 4 plastic glasses, large mixing bowl, 2 tablespoons, table knife, & chopping board.

Together

1. Spoon whipped cream & yoghurt into bowl & mix.

2. Chop banana into slices with table knife. & add to bowl.

3. Hold end of plastic bag shut while child squishes strawberries with hands until mushy.

4. Add mushed strawberries to bowl & lightly mix.

5. Break meringues into small pieces & put in bowl. Mix again.

6. Spoon mixture into plastic glasses & decorate with remaining quartered strawberries.

Raspberry Cheesecake

serves 6

My Mum used to make this cheesecake for us when we were little. I love how gentle the flavours are. My children now really enjoy it too, both the making and eating. You can make any flavour you like; simply use a different flavour of yoghurt. Will keep in an airtight container in fridge for 2-3 days.

Ingredients

- 100g (3 1/2oz) digestive biscuits (graham crackers)
- 50g (4tbsp) butter
- 75g (1/3cup) cream cheese
- 50g (3tbsp) sugar
- 140ml (2/3cup) double (heavy) cream
- 125g (1/2cup) raspberry yoghurt

Adult Prep

- Put digestive biscuits (graham crackers) into a plastic freezer bag.
- Gently melt butter & transfer to a jug.
- Whip 140ml cream or use ready-whipped.
- Lay out: 18-20cm round flan or cake tin (pan), rolling pin, 2 mixing bowls, 2 tablespoons & 2 wooden spoons.

Together

1 Hold end of freezer bag whilst child bashes it with rolling pin. Bash & squash until digestives look like breadcrumbs.

2 Put crushed biscuits in bowl. Pour on melted butter & mix with wooden spoon.

3 Put crumbs into cake tin. Press down with hands like building a sandcastle. Put tin in fridge.

4 Put cream cheese & sugar in other bowl. Mix thoroughly with wooden spoon.

5 Add whipped cream & yoghurt. Fold together with table spoon. Don't over mix.

6 Spoon mixture onto biscuit base and spread out with back of spoon.

And finally... chill in fridge for at least 2 hours.

raspberry cheesecake p52

banana & choc chip cakes p44

chocolate cake squares p50

cheese soufflé p57

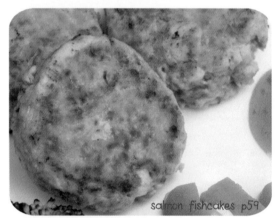
salmon fishcakes p59

cheese & bacon muffins p56

chicken & ham pie p58

Budding Little Chefs
for those ready for more of a challenge

Cheese & Bacon Muffins

makes 6 muffins or 9 cupcake size

Delicious savoury muffins for breakfast, lunch, or to take on a picnic. If you want to make a vegetarian option, substitute the bacon with 1 grated courgette (zucchini). Making them in muffin cases is good for adults, but I find the cupcake size better for children's appetites.

Adult Prep

- Cook rashers of bacon & leave to cool.
- Grate cheddar cheese.
- Preheat oven to 190C/375F/Gas5.
- Lay out: ingredients, 1 cupcake tray, 9 cupcake cases, large mixing bowl, medium mixing bowl, wooden spoon, 2 tablespoons & fork.

Ingredients

- 2 bacon rashers
- 125g (1 1/4cups) self-raising flour
- 100g (1 cup) cheddar cheese
- 1 small egg
- 50ml (1/4cup) milk
- 50ml (1/4cup) olive oil
- 50ml (1/4cup) tinned (canned) cream of mushroom soup

Together

1. Put cases into trays & set aside.

2. Tear cooked bacon rashers into little pieces & put in large mixing bowl..

3. Add flour & grated cheese. Mix with wooden spoon.

4. Break egg into medium bowl. Add milk, olive oil & mushroom soup. Whisk with fork until combined.

5. Add wet mixture to dry ingredients & mix with wooden spoon until just combined.

6. Spoon mixture into muffin or cupcake cases until about 2/3 full.

And finally... bake for 20 minutes (cupcake size) or 25 minutes (muffin size).

Cheese Soufflé

serves 4

I was in two minds whether to include this recipe because it won't suit every child. They will need to be gentle, get their hands into raw egg and use an electric whisk. I have included it because it is do-able for an older toddler and an exciting challenge for the super keen little chef. They love to watch it puff up like magic in the oven.

Adult Prep

- Finely chop parsley.
- Grate cheddar cheese.
- Preheat oven to 190C/375F/Gas 5.
- Lay out: ingredients, 2 large mixing bowls, small mixing bowl, hand whisk, electric whisk, straight-sided oven-proof 1.5 litre dish & tablespoon.

Ingredients

- 6 eggs
- 190ml (1 cup) milk
- 2 tablespoons parsley
- 30g (4tbsp) plain (all-purpose) flour
- Small pinch of salt
- Small pinch of paprika
- Dash of Worcestershire sauce
- 90g (1 cup) cheddar cheese

Together

1. Break egg into small bowl. "Scoop" out egg yolk with hands & run it over fingers to separate egg white.

2. Put yolk in one large bowl & white in other. Repeat with each egg. If a yolk breaks, do not use it.

3. Add milk, flour, parsley, salt, paprika & Worcestershire sauce to yolks & mix with hand whisk. Add cheese.

4. Electric whisk egg whites until turn white & a peak forms when you lift whisk.

5. Stir 1/3 of whites into yolk mix. Add rest of whites & gently fold in. Don't over mix to keep it fluffy.

6. Pour into straight-sided dish.

And finally... bake in oven for 40 minutes. Serve immediately before it deflates.

Chicken & Ham Pie

serves 4

I love this recipe for using up leftover chicken and ham. It does involve rolling, but if your child is too young to use a rolling pin, you can use ready-rolled puff pastry. I use a handle herb chopper so that my children can help me prepare the parsley.

Adult Prep

- Finely chop parsley.
- Preheat oven to 210F/410C/Gas 7.
- Lay out: ingredients, 1 litre pie dish, large mixing bowl, wooden spoon, tablespoon, teaspoon, fork, rolling pin, chopping board, pastry brush, cookie cutters in fun shapes (optional) & small bowl.

Ingredients

- 200g (7oz) cooked chicken
- 150g (3/4cup) cooked ham
- 100g (1 cup) mushrooms
- 200ml (1 cup) tinned (canned) cream of chicken soup
- Tablespoon parsley
- 230g (8oz) puff pastry
- Flour for dusting
- 1 egg

Together

1. Tear chicken, ham & mushrooms into small pieces & put in large bowl.

2. Pour in cream of chicken soup & parsley & mix. Spoon into pie dish & set aside.

3. Dust flour on chopping board & rolling pin. Roll pastry into rough circle, big enough to cover pie dish.

4. Place pastry on top of chicken mixture. Press down gently around the edge.

5. Pull off excess pastry & use to mould fun shapes with hands or cookie cutters. Put on pie to decorate.

6. Whisk egg with fork in small bowl. Brush egg over pie with pastry brush.

And finally... bake in oven for 25 minutes until golden brown.

Salmon Fishcakes

makes 8 small cakes

An easy, tasty fishcake recipe, which is another family favourite. I use a handle grater and herb chopper so my children can help prepare the cheese and parsley.

Adult Prep

- Open tin (can) of salmon & drain off liquid.
- Grate cheddar cheese.
- Finely chop parsley.
- Lay out: ingredients, mixing bowl, fork, tablespoon, child-safe scissors, plate or chopping board.

Ingredients

- x2 170g (5oz) tins (cans) boneless salmon
- 2 spring onions (scallions)
- 1 egg
- 30g (1/2cup) breadcrumbs
- 1/2 tablespoon Worcestershire sauce
- 1 tablespoon sweet chilli sauce
- 20g (1/4cup) cheddar cheese
- Tablespoon parsley
- 2 tablespoons plain (all-purpose) flour

Together

1. Put salmon into mixing bowl & fork through or break up with hands.

2. Cut spring onions into little pieces with child-safe scissors & put in bowl.

3. Break an egg into the bowl & mix with fork.

4. Add breadcrumbs, Worcestershire sauce, sweet chilli sauce, parsley & cheese. Mix.

5. Once well combined, use hands to shape 8 fish cakes & place on plate or board.

6. Sprinkle flour over both sides.

And finally... chill in fridge for minimum 20 minutes to stop them breaking up on cooking. Fry gently in oil for about 3-4 minutes each side.

Pea & Ham Quiche: Pastry

Serves 4

Shortcrust pastry is a fun, easy pastry for a budding little chef to learn and can be used to make all sorts of things, including quiches. I have split the recipe into two parts. You could do them both consecutively. Or, I find it works well to do the pastry in one session and then the filling in another. You can keep the pastry as an uncooked ball (step 3) wrapped in cling-film (wrap) in the fridge for 2-3 days. Or you could freeze - just make sure you defrost completely before using.

Ingredients

- 140g (1 1/4 cups) plain (all-purpose) flour plus some for dusting
- Small pinch of salt
- 65g (2 1/4oz) unsalted butter
- 35ml water

Adult Prep

- Preheat oven to 200C/390F/Gas 6.
- Lay out: ingredients, large mixing bowl, board or mat for rolling on, rolling pin, tin foil, 18cm flan tin (pan), table knife, chopping board & fork.

Together

1. Cut butter into rough 1 cm cubes using table knife.

2. Put flour, salt & butter cubes into bowl. Rub butter into flour using finger tips until looks like breadcrumbs.

3. Sprinkle over water. Squeeze together with hands to make a ball of pastry.

4. Dust flour over board & rolling pin to prevent sticking. Roll pastry into rough circle about 2-3mm thick.

5. Lay pastry over flan tin. Lightly press into sides leaving pastry to overlap over top. Do not trim off excess.

6. Use fork to prick holes in base. Loosely crumple 4 pieces of tin foil into large balls & put on base.

Bake for 15 minutes. Set aside ready for filling.

serves 4

This part of the recipe can be done by a younger toddler. So if you want to make a quiche with a child who is not yet ready for pastry, do part 1 yourself (or with an older child), or use a pre-cooked shortcrust pastry base. Serve warm or cold. Will keep in an airtight container in fridge for 3 days.

Ingredients

- 3 eggs
- 120ml (3/8cup) single (half/half) cream
- 120g (1/2cup) frozen peas
- 60g (1/2cup) grated cheddar cheese
- 60g (1/2cup) ham
- Salt & pepper

Adult Prep

- Preheat oven to 190C/375F/Gas 5.
- Grate cheddar cheese.
- Lay out: ingredients, large mixing bowl & fork.

Together

1 Break eggs into large bowl. Whisk with fork.

2 Tear ham into small pieces & add to bowl.

3 Add cream, peas, cheese & small pinch of salt & pepper. Mix well with fork.

4 Pour mixture into cooked pastry base

And finally... bake in oven for 40-45 minutes until set. Run a sharp knife around top of flan tin to remove excess pastry.

apple & blackberry crumble p63

pea & ham quiche p60

Apple & Blackberry Crumble

serves 6

Apple crumble is my eldest daughter's favourite dessert, so I had to find a way for her to cook it. I use an 'apple master' that peels, cores and cuts apples by turning a handle. This makes the apple preparation much quicker and means my daughter can help. Serve warm or cold with cream, ice cream or custard. Will keep in an airtight container in fridge for 3 days.

Ingredients

- 4 dessert apples
- 100g blackberries
- 75g (2 1/2oz) butter
- 175g (1 1/4cups) plain (all-purpose) flour
- 50g (3tbsp) sugar
- 1/8 teaspoon ground cinnamon (optional)

Adult Prep

- Peel, core & cut 4 dessert apples into slices.
- Preheat oven to 220C/425F/Gas 7.
- Lay out: ingredients, oven-proof dish, large mixing bowl, tablespoon, table knife & chopping board.

Together

1 Lay out apple slices in oven-proof dish. Add blackberries, spacing them out. Set aside.

2 Cut butter into approximately 1 cm cubes with table knife.

3 Put flour & butter cubes into bowl. Rub butter into flour using finger tips until looks like breadcrumbs.

4 Add sugar & if using, cinnamon. Stir with tablespoon.

5 Spoon crumble mixture on top of apples & blackberries, spreading it out evenly.

And finally... bake in oven for 30 minutes until light brown.

Bread & Butter Pudding

serves 4

This basic bread & butter pudding is one of my favourites because you can easily experiment with it. You can spread jam or marmalade on the bread as well as the butter. Or try adding fruit and/or substituting the raisins with chocolate chips. Serve warm or cold. Will keep in an airtight container in fridge for 3 days.

Ingredients

- 25g (2tbsp) butter
- 3 slices of bread
- 1 egg
- 250ml (2 1/2cups) milk
- 50g (1/4cup) sugar
- 75g (1/2cup) raisins
- 1/8 teaspoon ground cinnamon (optional)

Adult Prep

- Remove butter from fridge at least 1 hour before using to soften.
- Preheat oven to 190C/375F/Gas 5.
- Lay out: ingredients, oven-proof dish, large mixing bowl, fork, plate or mat & table knife.

Together

1. Spread butter on bread. Cut each slice diagonally into 4 triangles.

2. Overlap triangular bread slices in bottom of ovenproof dish.

3. 'Hide' raisins under bread slices

4. Put egg, milk, sugar & cinnamon in bowl. Mix well with fork.

5. Pour mixture onto bread slices.

6. Squish down bread with fork.

And finally... bake in oven for 35 minutes until set.

Chocolate Chip Cookies

makes 12 cookies

Cookies are a wonderfully forgiving biscuit to make with young children. I have included the classic chocolate chip version, but you can get creative to make all sorts of different versions. Substitute chocolate chips with raisins and add a pinch of ground cinnamon for a fruity cookie. The variations are endless. Will keep in an airtight container for up to a week.

Adult Prep

- Take butter out of fridge at least 1 hour before using to soften.
- Preheat oven to 180C/350F/Gas 4.
- Lay out: ingredients, baking tray, greaseproof (waxed) paper or baking mat, large mixing bowl, wooden spoon, 2 tablespoons & cooling rack.

Ingredients

- 140g (5oz) unsalted butter
- 75g (1/3cup) demerara sugar
- 75g (1/3cup) sugar
- 1 egg
- 170g (1 3/4cup) plain (all-purpose) flour
- 1/4 teaspoon salt
- 3/4 teaspoon bicarb of soda (baking soda)
- 200g (1 1/4cup) chocolate chips

Together

1. Place greaseproof paper or baking mat on baking tray. Set aside.

2. Squish & stir butter, brown sugar and sugar with wooden spoon until combined.

3. Break egg into mixture & mix until combined.

4. Add flour, salt, bicarbonate of soda & chocolate chips & mix.

5. Scoop and scrape tablespoon dollops of cookie dough, spaced out onto baking tray.

And finally... bake in oven for 15 minutes until golden but still soft. Allow to cool for 5 minutes on tray then transfer to cooling rack.

Jam Swirl

serves 4

The trickier part of Jam Swirl is making the pastry. If you use ready-made rolled shortcrust pastry (250g) or make the pastry yourself in advance then even very young toddlers would enjoy making this. You can eat warm with cream as a pudding or cut into thin slices whilst still warm and eat cold as biscuits (cookies). Will keep in an airtight container for 5 days.

Ingredients

- 2 heaped tablespoons jam
- 150g (1 1/2cups) plain (all-purpose) flour, plus some for dusting
- 90g (3oz) butter
- 1 egg

Adult Prep

- Preheat oven to 170C/325F/Gas 3.
- Lay out: ingredients, table knife, chopping board, large mixing bowl, small mixing bowl, fork, rolling pin, tablespoon & baking tray lined with greaseproof (waxed) paper or non-stick baking mat.

Together

1 Cut butter into rough 1 cm cubes using table knife.

2 Put flour & butter cubes into bowl. Rub butter into flour using finger tips until looks like breadcrumbs.

3 Whisk egg in small bowl with fork. Pour into large bowl & squeeze mix with hands to form pastry ball.

4 Dust flour over board & rolling pin to prevent sticking. Roll pastry into rough square 3-4mm thick.

5 Dollop 2 generous tablespoonfuls of jam onto pastry square. & spread out.

6 Carefully roll-up pastry. Press down ends to seal in jam. Put on tray.

And finally... bake in oven for 40 minutes until golden brown.

Mini Fruity Scones

makes 14 mini scones

This is a variation on my husband's Gran's scone recipe. She used to flatten the dough into a lined cake tin (pan) to make one giant scone, which she then cut into slices to serve. However, these mini versions make a great tea-time treat or snack. If you want plain scones, just leave out the currants.

Adult Prep

- Preheat oven to 190C/375F/Gas 7.
- Lay out: ingredients, mixing bowl, wooden spoon, 48mm round cookie cutter, pastry brush, baking tray lined with greaseproof (waxed) paper or non-stick baking mat, table knife & chopping board.

Ingredients

- 60g (5tbsp) butter
- 225g (2 1/4cups) self-raising flour
- 25g (2tbsp) sugar
- Pinch of salt
- 50g (1/3cup) currants
- 100ml (1/2cup) milk
- 10ml (2tbsp) milk for brushing tops
- 2 tbsp plain (all-purpose) flour for dusting

Together

1 Cut butter into rough 1 cm cubes using table knife.

2 Put flour & butter cubes into bowl. Rub butter into flour using finger tips until looks like breadcrumbs.

3 Add sugar, currants and pinch of salt. Mix with wooden spoon.

4 Add milk & mix. Bring together with hands until you have a lump of dough.

5 Dust board with flour. Roughly flatten out dough with hands to about 1.5-2cm thick.

6 Cut circles with cutter. Put on baking tray & paint tops with milk using pastry brush.

And finally... bake in oven for 15 minutes until light brown. If you're doing Gran Oxford's Giant Scone, bake for an extra 5 minutes.

bread & butter pudding p64

mini fruity scones p67

chocolate chip cookies p65

jam swirl p66

Toddlers with Allergies

Allergies to things like milk-protein and egg are more prevalent in very young children. So the chances are that some of you are cooking with toddlers with allergies. Here is a table to help you find the recipes you can do:

go for it | **avoid** | **ok with adjustments**

Recipe	Dairy Allergy	Egg Allergy
Apple & Blackberry Crumble	use dairy-free spread	
Apple Cake	use dairy-free spread	
Banana & Choc Chip Cakes	use dairy-free spread	leave out egg
Bread & Butter Pudding		
Cheese & Bacon Muffins		
Cheese Soufflé		
Chicken & Ham Pie		
Chicken Bread Baskets		fill with salmon paste
Chocolate Biscuit Cake	grease tin with oil	
Chocolate Cake	use water not milk; use icing or jam - not spread	leave out eggs
Chocolate Chip Cookies	use dairy-free spread & raisins	
Chocolate Fork Biscuits	use dairy-free spread	
Curried Chicken Wraps		

Allergy table continued...

	go for it	avoid	ok with adjustments

	Dairy Allergy	Egg Allergy
Frittata		
Frozen Yoghurt Lollies		
Fruity Mess		
Fruity Yoghurt Pots		
Guacamole		
Ham & Mushroom Pizza	leave out cheese	
Jam Swirl	use dairy-free spread	use 2-3tbsp water not egg
Mini Fruity Scones		
Pea & Ham Quiche		
Rainbow Salad	leave out cheese	
Raspberry Cheesecake		
Salmon Fishcakes	leave out cheese	leave out egg
Salmon Paste		
Sausage Pasta Bake	leave out cheese	
Shortbread	use dairy-free spread	
Tuna Mayo Pitta Pockets	leave out cheese	
Vegetable Samosas		

Limiting Waste

I hate wasting food both for environmental and cost reasons. I have intentionally duplicated ingredients in multiple recipes so that if you have something left over, you can use it up on another day in another recipe. I have also included several recipes to use up things like leftover meat and vegetables. Here is a list to help you find what you can cook depending on what you have available or need to use up.

Apples
    Apple & Blackberry Crumble
    Apple Cake

Blueberries
    Fruity Mess
    Fruity Yoghurt Pots
    Rainbow Salad

Bananas
    Banana & Choc Chip Cakes
    Fruity Mess
    Fruity Yoghurt Pots

Bread
    Bread & Butter Pudding
    Chicken Bread Baskets
    Salmon Fishcakes
    Salmon Paste

Cheddar Cheese
    Cheese & Bacon Muffins
    Cheese Soufflé

Cheddar Cheese cont.
    Frittata
    Pea & Ham Quiche
    Salmon Fishcakes
    Sausage Pasta Bake
    Tuna Mayo Pitta Pockets

Chicken (cooked)
    Chicken Bread Baskets
    Curried Chicken Wraps
    Chicken & Ham Pie

Chocolate Chips
    Banana & Choc Chip Cakes
    Chocolate Chip Cookies

Cream
    Apple & Blackberry Crumble
    Apple Cake
    Frozen Yoghurt Lollies
    Fruity Mess
    Raspberry Cheesecake
    Salmon Paste

Currants/Raisins
- Bread & Butter Pudding
- Mini Fruity Scones

Digestive Biscuits
- Chocolate Biscuit Cake
- Fruity Yoghurt Pots
- Raspberry Cheesecake

Eggs
- Apple Cake
- Banana & Choc Chip Cakes
- Bread & Butter Pudding
- Cheese & Bacon Muffins
- Cheese Soufflé
- Chicken & Ham Pie
- Chocolate Cake Squares
- Chocolate Chip Cookies
- Frittata
- Pea & Ham Quiche
- Salmon Fishcakes

Cooked Ham
- Chicken & Ham Pie
- Ham & Mushroom Pizza
- Pea & Ham Quiche
- Rainbow Salad

Mango Chutney
- Curried Chicken Wraps
- Vegetable Samosas

Mozzarella Cheese
- Ham & Mushroom Pizza
- Rainbow Salad

Salmon (tinned/canned)
- Salmon Paste
- Salmon Fishcakes

Sweetcorn (tinned/canned)
- Rainbow Salad
- Tuna Mayo Pitta Pockets

Tomato Sauce (Ready-made)
- Ham & Mushroom Pizza
- Sausage Pasta Bake

Yoghurt (Flavoured)
- Cheesecake
- Frozen Yoghurt Lollies

Yoghurt (Greek)
- Curried Chicken Wraps
- Frozen Yoghurt Lollies
- Fruity Yoghurt Pots

Vegetables (mixed, cooked)
- Frittata
- Vegetable Samosas

Index

Acknowledgements

Thank you to my editing team: Nathalie Paterson, Sarah Paterson, Kate Cole and Anne Woolmer for their meticulous checking. And to my parents and brothers for their enduring support and input.

Thank you Emily Black, Hannah Bennett, Jackie Cruise, Alex Ginn, Emma Hawkins, and their children for your invaluable feedback. Thank you Angela Bastable and Sue Pankow for passing on some of your years of child-care wisdom.

Thank you to all those friends and toddlers who have tested recipes. And thank you Eve and Zoe for being my ultimate guinea pigs and inspiration.

And finally, the most important thank you must go to my husband, John; the brains behind the visual aspects of this book, my harshest critic and my greatest champion. Thank for all the late nights and weekends you gave up. I could never have done it without you.